Re-M

MW00935176

Poems of Earth and Soul

Advance Praise for Re-Membering

"Grandfather knew to 'Look out for rattlesnakes and rusted nails' and he also knew what too many have forgotten, the primacy of the earth and our place with her. Ryan Van Lenning's poems restore what's been lost to our souls, knowledge and love that was once considered basic and obvious. Poems are the perfect form for this remembering— Van Lenning takes us back to mud, to fire, roots and leaves, restoring what our species will not get far without."

–Patrice Vecchione, author of *Step into Nature: Nurturing Imagination and Spirit in Everyday Life*

———

"Ryan's poetry speaks deeply and clearly to the awakening to our true interconnected nature, which is the only way we can transform our world."

–Molly Young Brown, author of *Coming Back to Life: The Updated Guide to the Work That Reconnects* (co-authored with Joanna Macy), Editor of *Deep Times: A Journal of the Work That Reconnects*

———

"Ryan's poetry sprouts out of him from moist, fertile soil – painting a lush landscape of sensual and philosophical magic. His poems transport you to a way of living in relationship with the earth that is lovingly intimate. Ryan integrates body, spirit, and social commentary into a vision of how to live a nature-inspired life amidst noise and overrun technology."

–Ariana Candell, LMFT, The Earthbody Institute

———

"While every element of nature shows up colorful and free as its own self, it's rare these days to find a human animal who does the same. Ryan Van Lenning has really lived the words and stories that he writes into his poems. He's traveled the inner and outer wild places that feature in his poetry and he knows them well."

–Katie Baptist, LCSW, Co-Founder of Wild Nature Heart

Re-Membering: Poems of Earth and Soul

Ryan Van Lenning

 **WILD NATURE HEART PRESS**

WildNatureHeart.com

Dedicated to the Big Play,
the Sacred Ear,
and Deep Memory

Behind the breastbone
at the bottom of the yearn
lives the poetry
making the world wider
as it takes a deep breath

INTRODUCTION

It might be said that the most pressing challenge facing humanity is not climate chaos, not disappearing species and ecosystems in the 6th Great Extinction, not power-mad autocrats, not the degradation of the very concept of truth in our mass media and civic life, not global hunger or violent conflict over resources or ideology—though all these threaten to overwhelm us, indeed, threaten our very survival. Rather, these are all symptoms and signals, and what might be the root of all of those is a Great Forgetting.

It appears that modernity has drunk deeply from the fathomless River Lethe, the great underground river of oblivion, and as a consequence has forgotten a great number of important things about what it means to be a human being. Among them: an aligned relationship with our earth home and all our relations, one based on reciprocity and a profound sense of belonging, a fully alive embodiment of our wonderfully sense-based and sensual mammal bodies, and—though it is not popular to talk about it in these extremely unsoulful times—our soul and its callings. Nothing too abstract is meant by soul, but simply our rooted place in the scheme of things and the inimitable way each individual unfurls and embodies their psyche into the world.

A Great Remembering is not the only thing needed to reach the other side of critical problems facing humanity, but it doubtful it can be accomplished without it. The crisis of meaning which haunts our current cultural and psychic landscape and which lurks behind the endless distractions, addictions, and acting out is really the same problem by a different name.

The how and why and when of the Great Forgetting is open to debate and not the subject of this book, nor even something that poetry might excavate.

But what poetry might do is spark a remembering, to catalyze a spark in the dark that makes one gasp, "Oh, I remember that!" And thus begin a path of recovery.

Poetry then, like other art, can have an ecological and immunological function. Wild nature has been my intimate partner in creation. It is always there to jog our memory—to whisper, to sing, or sometimes to yell, "Hey, remember your childhood curiosity and wonder? Your innate creativity? Remember your senses and your wild animal sensuality? Remember your great love affair with the earth? Remember how to breathe deep and play? Remember your inimitable self, the one that sparked without shame or restriction?"

The poems in *Re-Membering* hope to evoke this gasp of memory.

To re-member is not only to recall in the mind the treasures that have been lost to forgetfulness, but to re-integrate the body, putting the members of our whole selves back together, and to re-belong ourselves to the vast and beautiful and endlessly fecund home we call earth, to become full members again in the great earth community.

YES, MEMORY

A Prayer for Remembering

I open all my ears
and hear the forgotten things.

The raptor in me opens his eyes.
The worm in me digs and feeds the roots.
The tree in me whispers slow green and golden syllables.
The nest in the limb, the egg in the nest, the bird in the egg,
the pulse in the bird.
The heart at the heart brings them together.

Seeing the spectrum,
I know the landscape from deep red to magenta
and feel the texture of each shade of love.

The contours and rhythms unfold clearly.
No less the sound than light.
No less the love, than both, I trust the whole.
I see the gossamer threads connecting.

I see the shining shadows, beautiful sacred wounds.
I see the hooks with compassion, both my own and others.
Like a man walking from dawn to noon,
I eat the long shadow into myself.
The wind is not silent and I am the river
wanting to be created through me.

I settle into the notes that are humming
or pitch my perfect harmony, expanding new measures
with the momentum of their own unfolding.

I know who I am.

When asked for the single thing, I said:
I remember.

The First Faraway

Grandfather said, "Look out
for rattlesnakes and rusted nails"

but we went in anyway
embarking on a bold adventure

without provisions of any kind
or shoes even

for what do they have to do
with an explorer's heart?

not in defiance, mind you
but only because we couldn't bare

not to let our bare feet
have an original conversation

with the soft duff of the pine grove
watching us…waiting for us…

we went in anyway, and later,
when we'd mapped all the new territories

when we'd squeezed a lifetime
from the rind of dawn to dusk

when the slant of the sun warns
of the docking of the day

when the reds and the browns
and the gregarious greens of the world

had covered us from shin to shiny face

and the exhaustion of our vast
explorer bodies starts to buzz

we anointed ourselves in the cold creek
flowing through the inexhaustible wilderness

watching us…waiting for us…

where we were the First Builders
Masters of tree forts, architects of forest villages

The Original Hunters
chasing raccoons and ravens

Primordial shamans burying owl feathers and dog bones
to ward off those cursed rattlesnakes

that were just around the next tree
watching us….waiting for us…

We were the First Explorers
lost for days within a single day

adrift on an evergreen raft
fueled by wild nature hearts

because we went in anyway
charting endless bright lands

on a small Iowa farm—
the first nearby faraway

watching us…waiting for us…

When Mud Was Our Friend

Remember when we used to run toward the rain
back when we were in love with the world
and it returned the favor?

When we couldn't
let raindrops fall to the ground
without our tongues
getting in on the action

or pass a body of water
a pile of leaves
without jumping in
and mud was our friend?

When shin bruises
arms drawn with scratches
numb fingers from staying out too long
were love bites from the world

and just the clouds in the sky
could evoke a song?

Now, is it that our only sunset
is the one that's a perfect 2×4
through The Device
with Lo-Fi filter that we heart?

Our only storm the one
we can prepare for adequately
informed three days hence?

The only mud found
on our Goodyear tires?

No mud shalt touch thy feet!
proclaims the commandment of maturity

I've heard that once in a while
a moon comes out to play in the sky

But to see her you have to put some things away

I don't know if it's true,
but I might take a peek this month

I just might even try
to run towards some things

Blue Pocket of Your Memory

By the nose and fingertips
and the slow bone of the heart—

It's how we'll begin to remember
all the things

that got swept away by the river
of forgetting

Let each person you meet be a path
beyond forgetfulness

Let each rock you feel be a road
of recovery

paved with those exquisite shards
from the original explosion

and putting them in the blue pocket
of your memory

Where I Get the News

"It is difficult to get the news from poems,
yet men die miserably every day,
for lack of what is found there."
—William Carlos Williams (from Asphodel, That Greeny Flower)

I get all my news from the fire that burns
at the edge of the dark, the place where I learn

I turn on the program, 'The Scent of the Wind'
and listen to all of the news that it sends

The roots and the leaves and the bark of the trees
have taught me how to be silent and free

The messages come from the river that flows
deserving all credit for all that I know

Consulting the spectrum of all of the hues
the network of colors where I get all the news

I get the reports from invisible threads
connecting the cores of the living and dead

I get all my news from the stone on the ground
from whom I've received any wisdom I've found

I get all my news from the fire that burns
at the edge of the dark, the place where I learn

The Old Names Don't Call Me

Let's talk about change.

Of all 50 states
the landscape of my homeland
is the most transformed

tiled and squared
skinned and gutted
hooked and hunted

the old farm is gone
the old school is paved
the old house is buried under rubble
the old rivers poisoned

The old names composted
and don't call me any more
and perhaps that's why everybody's confused

and though my roots have grown deeper now
I'd like to think
some of my many meandered feet
still have dirt on them
from the old land
which never went anywhere

Do you remember me heartland sun?
The way you used to turn me red?

Do you remember river run,
the way my skin would swim you in?

How about you, soil black?
Swinging bridge? Welcome back?

I have new names now
and it is difficult to forgive for that

it sticks in the wind of their throats

my names of yesterday
are tiny creek
and gentle breeze

today they're roaring rivers rainbow black
and eagle worm on western winds

my accent runs thick
as the Iowa River

I seek translations

but like biting flies
they're always escaping me

On My 86th Birthday

When I sit in the evening light
there are no cakes or candles

But a round pile of blueberries
From the two bushes that survived the winter

Bless the center of the cedar table
We made together at the dawn of our path

The size of marbles!
You would say

Now, looking out the stone-framed window
From my bed that faces the widening sea

My blood runs bright with memories
Of all the journeys

It's the ones I didn't take that weigh
Heavy upon me and clot me up

They seem more difficult
Than the ones where I came out the other side

I wish I would have greeted the dawn more
And jumped in the water

Without thought of who would see
My ordinary naked body

I didn't call my folks enough
Or tell my friends I loved them

To the women - did I thank you?
A hundred times I thank you

With each falling leaf I thank you
I'm sorry our wounds sometimes caused more pain

I hope you had rich, colorful lives
That love hugged you in the final moments

Sometimes I hurt you
Sometimes I hurt myself

Sometimes I didn't know how to connect
Or find the words

I built this room with my own hands
with stones from the creek

That we used to dip our feet in
Through all the seasons

Meeting months of sunsets
With sweat and peace and the tenderness

But now, I no longer need it
So I give it to you and you

And hope you enjoy
It as much as I have

If my legs were alive,
I'd jump like my 8-year old self

In a pile of leaves
The colors of an autumn blast

Yes, I still dream of running
But I'm content with the dream I lived

Yet still the questions pour through me:
Did I explore the sparks?

Did I follow my curiosity
and lean into all the fears?

Did I share my gifts
and open more than I closed?

And if my eyes weren't now masked like midnight
I'd look into the ox daisy of your eyes

I'd study the tiny hairs on your arm
How the light makes of them a forest

Delicate in the slant of the dipping sun
One last time

And not think of the words pomegranate
Or violet or any far-flung hue

But touch is still my finest tool
So merely place your long-loved hand in mine

Let us embrace
And feel the final fading

Of the warmth
Behind the darkening hills

Ship of Remembering

Have you ever forgotten?

The keys, the number, the lists?

The important things? Your body and your dream
and where the well was?

That image in your bones? The direction of your ship?

If you know that you have forgotten,
you're nearly there.

But if you have forgotten you have forgotten
you are in Deep

The river of forgetfulness has become a flood
your ship is in pieces, joining the others.

You grab a hold of any piece of debris
tossed atop the waves.

To get a breath.

Did you become convinced you were here to float like debris?

You are not here to float like debris—
You are here to remember who you are
so you can be medicine for us all,
a stunning fragment of the Dream
dreaming us whole.

It is not selfish to let go of the debris
in order to re-build your ship of remembering.

Keep following whatever allows you to grab a scrap of your own—
not theirs—to piece together your extravagant vessel.

The swallow does not mimic the eagle
the eagle does not flicker like the lizard
and the lizard and the lichen have distinct paths.

They do not drink of the river of forgetfulness
and in their stillness is the total movement of their life

The stillness is where the remembering begins—
Your ears open and hear the things:

It may sound like the whistle of the swallows.
Or the hummingbird's wings thrumming the air.
It may be the breeze through the needles.

Or the thunderous beat of a heart you had forgotten.
It may be the shattering imperative of your thunderbolt soul.

However it is—stay with it.
Listen so deep and richly you become the big ear
remembering all

Then, with what you hear
sail your beautiful preposterous ship
into the big dream

YES, MORNING

And Again It Begins

And you have the rest of the day
to fit in

and make your face do the things
that other faces do

and your mouth utter all the things
that aren't your own

So why not take this silent blue moment
with the heron

to wake up the day together
with your true face of delight?

The stale masks will still be there
hanging on the wall at noon

alongside the others
judgment and disappointment

In the afternoon you can follow
the story of the others

Who are following someone else's story
and in the evening you can join

the others in that ancient ritual
of draining the light from your eyes

But for now, put in your eyes
of dawn and dew

and let your bright peace
unveil itself as the fog recedes

Your bones and what holds them up
have been waiting so long for it

The night's last star doesn't seem to mind
and the day's star might even join you

Nothing Between You and the Song of Dawn

Sometimes the storm comes
to reclaim the things only borrowed

and washes the ground
from under your feet

that cold night took one leg
and the river took another

until half your roots
sailed to sea

yet you flourish deliciously
picking up rocks with your toes

and let birds play
in your time-worn beard

nothing will come between
you and the song of dawn

for you have a contract
with the world of change

swirling and opening
opening and swirling skyward

gnarled knuckles bowing to earth
fingers caressing the sky

The Many-Gathering Things

Dedicated to Mom

Those were the days I slept in
past when the day had swept in
and grinned. But then
I found what had commenced and gone,
past retrieval, past the dawn.

The many-gathering things had fled
while still I slept in my bed, but

the image of her sitting sits
in my bones and sitting yet—
the woman from which I came
at door of dawn and garden met.

Not doing, but the resting in the being
with the beings best
who at day break bring their
radiant zest.

First dew before warmth fell in
the inchèd crawl of light begins
the lavender, approaching thin
tumbled through distant cloud, now became
persimmon, pink, and rose-filled same

Among the marvels I had missed, she said
amidst the meandered mist, ahead
were many feathered friends in flight
or simply perched to sing the light
ten and five by her own eyes
different types, from land and skies

robin, warbler, cardinal, jay,
hummingbird, thrush, bush bird greys,

common corvid, hawk, and owl,
woodpecker, wren, and water fowl
but one that brought such joy to soul,
the black and orangèd Oriole.

She penned them in her notebook list
that in which she keeps them all
gathered in as dreams persist
that might be lost, not seen at all
unless one sits and in sitting gets
the blessings of the morning met.

Those were the days I slept in
and missed the things that dawn had sent.

But now I greet the light and flight
and fog and song and scent and sight
and have within that image bold
of her awake in morning's fold
inviting all the sounds that sing,
the rhythms of the bells that ring,
with the light that brings
the many-gathering things.

The Dawn Needs Me

Dear ones,

I must go now.

The dawn needs me uninterrupted.

Morning misses the feel of my face
across her feathered fingers.

The cool sage of her early breath
requires my participation.

Oh, how even through
the 101 impenetrable walls
of your comfortable palace
the cries of a forgotten land
carry like bugles of a victory march

A celebration of peace after the great war.

And though the heavy eyelids
of all your enchanting veils
conspire to hide
the gaze of the beloved

I must keep my promise
to the light—
she needs my eyes open
now more than ever

for shadows are racing
across the body of the world

and without my skin
as a witness
how can it stretch itself awake
and bring those shadows home?

The warbler needs my ears
to help summon the sun

The patient heart of the oaks
long for me to join
their silent morning meditations

So I must go now.

I climb the palace walls
and keep walking.

Past the courtyard, past the gate.

Across the belly of the golden fields.

If you should miss me
know I am doing my best
to help the dawn
spill herself recklessly
into the memory of our great belonging.

YES, BODIES

My Skin, Your Skin, Body Electric

My body is in an open relationship
with sun and grass,
the wind, the mud.

My marrow the mountains
my skin your skin
my belly the beast
my fertile fingertips ferned
delicate and alive

Roll your palms slowly across mine
and feel the turning of the season within you.

On you.

With you.

I am Abundance spoken through the wild syllables of the flesh.

No false beat will keep me from you,
touching forever bodies electric.

Equinox

I lost my balance
on the first day of spring

wading in with caution…
but she wanted my whole body

so I fell into her with a crash

a splash unplanned
open river offering

a baptism singing spring

eager soul and skin again
finding equilibrium

Collateral Beauty

Not intending to
I found myself bent over
on hands and knees

face nose-deep
in the forest of pineapple weed
scooping up the sharp-sweet
candy coated sword of sensory delight

I was hooked by the nostrils—
that animal body I hang out with
was at it again
asking me to come along
for the ride

It's the way the dance arrives like wind
from out of no where
possessing my limbs
making me do things
no one in their right mind   would do

but everyone in their right body   would do
with the flow of their own wind

It's how I found a pair of antlers
and a pair of wings
My pair of legs led me to a pair of bears
my pair of eyes to a paradox

It's how I met coyote
and the goose that laid the golden egg
that hatched the gosling
that gave the feather
that's in my crooked cap

It's how the heart-shaped stone
at the bottom of the river
found its way to the altar
at the bottom of my well

It's how the scent of her skin
still clings to me
and my tongue still testifies
to the taste of her everything

It's why the palms of my hands
have beautiful bruises
from the drum slap
tap
rap
rhythming raucously without a why

It's how the seven new scratches
that decorate my arms and legs
are like tattoo trophies
won from finding the view
of the mountain
with moons and stars on its shoulders—
collateral beauty of a body
following its own path

So no, I don't mind coming along for the ride
when my body gets hooked
by the smells and shapes
of an endlessly rippling world

Be Brave Bold Robot

The sharp hum of the city
has the rabbit of my mind
overtaking the tortoise of my soul

I deduce I am still breathing
by the fact I am alive
or vice versa

A type of aliveness meant for the head
and bodies are mere obstacles
or things to be stuffed
and shuffled around

STIMULATE is the motto of this foreign land
keeping the beast thriving
and hungry for everything
but never satisfied

"Be brave bold robot"
is etched in concrete for the benefit of commuters
who can't remember what wild water feels like
on their skin
or what mud feels like
on their face

It's all shallows here
there's no profit in the depths
but my tortoise is drawing me
to the nearby faraway to seek water

I dig my feet in the sandy bank
like crabs fleeing danger
and overhear a fellow zombie saying
"the data points show that people…"

and it's clear—they'll have to invent a new chart
to read the data points of a late winter afternoon
along the river

Twenty-four birds, sixteen mistletoes
four shadows of geese fall on my face

A hundred poison hemlock
a hundred hoary mustard
and countless cockleburs—all an antidote
to concrete and sirens

From the data I conclude:
some kinds of prickliness are better than others

I join a cattle egret at his fishing hole
the sun warming our backs

I'm just brave enough to slow down a bit
to notice all the fish in the depths

The tortoise of my soul sticks his head out
and jumps

daring to join them

Smell of Joy

Have you ever seen the color
of the evening bird's song?

It smells like joy—one of the things they rarely print
in the park brochure.

It's different for everybody
But for me it's a spring breeze
floating an orange and turquoise shell
out of an ancient canyon

It's a red and yellow whistle
petaling through me like bubbles
splitting and swallowing themselves
out on the limbs of twilight tree.

That's the smell of joy—
which the brochures fail to mention.

They do mention to stay on the trails
but they don't say that
when you walk the fallen log
stretching from shore to shore
of the red forest

strange things happen

with the birds
and the scents
and the heart-bodies of the forest.

They also neglect to inform you
that that when you see
the 7am rays interplay
with the morning dew

hugging the gentle green arms of the old oak

you will have to change your life.

Sometimes the truth gets told
and they say "Enjoy the Park"

So you do.

The creek jumps up to kiss your face
and the smell of joy
floods your cells
and you know you will never leave.

Today I Pity the Gods

Today I pity the gods
and pure spirits
in their unearthly realms
without ferns or figs or falling rain

or autumn's aroma
among the oak-laurel lane

I mourn for what they
don't even know
they don't know
like the hint of salt on the scent of the sea
or the impossible colors
of the walnut tree

How sad they will never taste a wild blackberry
purchased with fingers stained
juice streaming down their chin
with a grin

What could their wings mean
without blue skies
compared to doves
and diving falcons?

Angelic skin without knowledge
of the caresses of warm wind
or warmer women?

Can their heart flutter like a bush bird
upon a lover's utterance?

What bleak void must their eyes
gaze out upon

that holds no horizon
overflowing with peach and promise

What could mark the
span of their days
in dreadful sunless time?

How lonely must they be
without the immeasurable elation
and unfathomable despair
of the human heart
to keep them company?

Bereft of both beauty and terror
of what, truly, could they be in awe?

YES, TREES

Trees Grow Out of My Body

Trees grow out of my body

I'm not sure if I planted them
or if they planted me

All I know is that
an oak tree grows behind my ears
soaking sunshine into my skull

Each time I take a breath
a nut falls from my sternum

A sapling takes the space between my toes
sending roots earthward
drinking up autumn rain
into my belly
awfully cold but refreshing

When the east wind blows
the canopy of my head sways gently
to the left   to the right

Do you catch my drift?

Buckeyes from my eyes—
Do you see what I'm saying?

Madrones out my fingertips—
Do you feel me?

They must think I'm soil
and I haven't tried to convince them otherwise

Bare Bones

Your flashy garments gone
And stripped austere you stand
Thrust extravagant your eager hands
In splashing persimmon-dawn.

Who but you owns your bones?
None other than sips your roots
Or with delicate fingers caress
The moments eternity loans.

Be not impatient for the buds
That flow from your marrow blood
But revel in your naked form
In the season's quiet flood.

Believe in your bones sincere
In quiet unadornéd dance
Who you are in winter
Is who you are all year.

Take A Right at the Bay Tree

Go down to the redwoods
walk through the tall dry poison hemlock

duck under the arched wild plum tree
and take an immediate right

Walking along the horsetail ferns
and blackberry-lined path
step over four sleepy
and moss-covered bay trees
and a right at the fifth

I'll be under the giant live oak

The doorbell is a purple thistle
but it's not very loud
so just knock on the trunk of my tree

If you get lost, inquire of the bunnies or owls
they'll know where to find me

Blush of the Flesh

The blush of the flesh
of the fruit of the limb

of the tree that she climbed
to get to the blush of the flesh

is born of the heat
of the meeting between

the sun and the skin
and the warmth of the heart within

First Syllable

In the middle of the forest
in that part of the dark
you ordinarily avoid

an old live oak lives
with lichen limbs
fern green and orange, and golden trimmed
a cozy jacket ember warm

Ki* has a name cannot be told

among the roots a beating heart
within ki's chambers
blood bright as stars
flowing beyond my sight and yours

within the blood
a flurry of birds
singing "Yes!" in all the words—
the first syllable flies and shouts

when a herd of deer steps out
of the flurried birds' mouths
you peer into the buzzing light
of each other's flighty eyes

suddenly you know that they know
that they are you, that you are they

and they will go back to mindless graze
fearless and forgetful and in a daze

as you will too

Whose blood is it?

Whose heart beats?

The Great Oak,
The Ancient Stone,
The Blessed Dark,
The One Beat,
The Cosmic Eye?

Who knows?

The Great Circulation
on and on and on

*Ki is a proposed alternative pronoun by Robin Wall Kimmerer to refer to people of the earth, to avoid objectification that comes with using "it" in the English language. See her exposition in Yes Magazine or in her brilliant and beautiful book, Braiding Sweetgrass: Indigenous Wisdom, Scientific Knowledge, and the Teachings of Plants

YES, SEASONS

My Heart Has Walked the Seasons

There are no strangers here any more

My heart has walked the seasons
with the rooted ones
conspiring to add a ring or two

I don't have to ask what time it is
yet spring is nearly an unbearable improbability
on everybody's door
a fragrant evangelist preaching resurrection

I stumbled through the brambled wounds
of the world thick as blackberries
and sunk a falcon's claw into the flurry

Though my beard grows with each whisper
of the eastern wind
and my robe is well-worn from a winter apprenticeship

I fear I don't have a meadow within
worthy enough to hold it all—this preposterous birth

Tonight I'll once again rest all our heads
under the inexhaustible moon
on a pillow of red dust
out-breath of the forest's meditation
spinning itself through the seasons
and grow the edges of my booming meadow,
letting the impossible rabbits feed

for not even the snowy plum refuses to blossom
when the spring breeze
sends her strange invitations

Fall Away

Hover here for a moment

in the balance between
darkness and light
between drawing within
and explosive expression

Harvest your juicy sun-soaked fruits
perhaps too easily procured

Honor the growing shadow

It's okay to grieve the dry and dying

Relish the transition
and let the leaves no longer needed
flitter to the floor

feeling the bright weight of the world
fall from your limbs

Two walnuts per hour:
that's the pace here

Thud!

With fingered leaves leaping
trying to outdo the laurel
with its yellow strikes
against blue October sky

Two walnuts per hour
greet the ground:

Wap!

Keeps me on track.

Tell the Truth About the Season

You can try to live summer in the winter
Or morning at midnight under the full moon
but eventually, the season is revealed.

It's Fall. The world takes a deeper breath and a sacred pause

It's raining yellow bay leaves and brown needles
in the redwoods
they've slipped on their autumn coats overnight
dropping yesterday to the ground like an old story
that no longer makes sense

They know when to let go
offering the best of their beauty
as gifts to the land and the next season,
each leaf an invitation
to follow our own turning

It's Fall.

The world takes a deeper breath and a sacred pause

We will harvest the things that can be harvested
But we know the things that must fall must fall
for the new ground to be prepared
with the composted remains
of what no longer serves

It's Fall. Can we finally tell the truth about the season?

In the midst of the big race,
the world takes a deeper breath and a sacred pause
while the leaves of the empire fall out of our hair
You know of which empire I speak

The one whose summer's shoulders brought
great gifts: all bright and fast and furious
and juicy and sexy and convenient.
And more. It always brought more.
Whether the more was what we needed or not

But it promised too much, took too much
and now the Great Descent has commenced
the Great Unraveling arrives like a sword of autumn

There will be a buttoning up
a shrinking of the afternoon
a shedding

It's a moment to tell the truth about.

Perhaps we fear winter
because we don't yet see what new spring awaits
but press your ear to the ground of your being
and you will hear:

seeds of the new dream
already planted in the soil
of our gentle, beating hearts
seeds of belonging planted in Deep Time

and we know
there's no way to spring
but through the lengthening dark and cold
and wet and unknowing

Let's tell the truth: it's Fall.

The world takes a deeper breath
and a sacred pause

A Currant Affair

A mid-winter warmth wins your hand
and draws you out for pendulous play
to blossom right in front of me
a dream of pink in light of day

Draw me in your inflorescence
Draw me in with all your senses
Draw me with sweet sagey scents and
Draw me in with rosy fervence

Fragrant is your dangling racemes
bunching grapelets of blushing dreams

Your pretty little grape does dangle
in morning dew at such an angle
I want to pluck but dare not do it
perhaps the spring brings ripened fruit

I want to be a tiny ant
and on my tongue take in the sweet
But I'll wait a little longer
and savor all your lovely treats

Coffee berry is your partner
the ruby-throated loves you too
a sparkle in the green and grey
a splash of color, a flashy hue

Grow in flow of warming current
purple berry in longer days
I want a taste, Sweetest Currant
before the birds take you away

How to Read a Poem About Spring

Stand up straight
and compose yourself

Clear your throat
and begin making a list of all the things
that signal the coming of spring

Things like first robins
longer days and sprouting buds

You might even find a daffodil
or bee on your list
but don't try to make them buzz

Certainly don't make your poppies sing
or your creeks talk

It is not necessary to lift your voice
on the western wind
when you describe the baby otter
having breakfast in the river

When you discuss the river
you can simply say it flows
and not import a fancy word like dance or meander

People know what rivers do
it is not necessary for you to dress it up
or to make your words smell like lavender

Are you suggesting you appreciate spring
more than anybody else?

Or you have some special way of seeing a river?

It is okay to say the sun rises,
we know that is shorthand for the truth
but if you start having some relationship
with something called the magical persimmon dawn
people won't take you seriously

A day is a dime a dozen
so don't swell up and round
like a soaring rain cloud
dropping hints of summer

If doves enter the picture
or an owl visits you
or the frogs return chirping

duly note it
but don't make a big show of it

It's not like it all hasn't happened before.

Catalogue the qualities that you call spring
like a grocery list—
one can of this, one package of that
ingredients of a season:

willow catkins
pink-flowering currants
nettles and horsetails
shorter nights
warmer days and such and such

Oh, and can you grab a fist full o' lupine?
I want to try a recipe
I saw on the back of a box

Read it carefully as if you were preparing
a report for the General Assembly
at the United Nations

Don't get excited about the black butterflies
with orange and blue spots
or burgundy dragonflies
flitting about

You don't have to flit about
you are not a butterfly
and if you pretend you are
things will just get confusing

So remember, you are merely documenting

You are collecting data to be compiled
and a non-binding resolution will be issued
on whether this indeed is spring
and if so, what happened and why

or whether spring is just another word
like smokestack or elaboration

Regardless, the fuchsia wild flowers are not there
for you to get a hard-on over

the skin of the madrone is not there
for you to cop a feel

use the Latin name *Arbutus menziesii*
if you need something to curb your enthusiasm
and if the bark was traditionally made into a tea
for medicinal purposes

that is an interesting fact

but don't put much effort into describing
how your heart leaped in childish joy at trying it

Just say, "it was bitter"
and people won't be tempted to try it themselves

Plum blossoms are generous with their scent
it serves a purpose

But it is embarrassing for you to be effusive
when it excites your nose

That is okay for a ten-year old
but you are not a ten-year old
you are a mature person

So stay calm and objective

people will respect you more
and that is what you are going for

When Summer Dives Like Fools for Gold

In heat as thick as brambles be
I say goodbye in deep July

When summer dives like fools for gold
with face in water crisp and cold
I say goodbye, and say it bold

Even as I'm saying hi
to sun so high, I say goodbye

Letting go while taking in
a way to stay awake again

With berries ripe as fat dog days
I say farewell, as they swell

with arms around the searing sun
and a tang on the tip of tongue
and the summer is yet young

I say so long, so long I say
Deep down in a summer day

Sip the Season Darkly

Darkness has arrived
wrapping its inky cloak
across the season of our lives

Long shadows and owls
stand tall and salute
Autumn's funeral song
becoming winter's march

asking us not to skip too quickly
over the hour
with an eager eye
grasping towards cherry blossoms
awaiting on the other side

Drink deeply from the season, they say,
and offer a cup overflowing
with the thick sweetness
from a darker vine

Sip the season darkly:
wisdom hidden from summer's glare
may yet pass our lips
should we have the thirst for it

sip the season's slow
inward night embrace
and listen for it

The Silence – can you hear it?

Is it not the dream of the dark womb
before the scream?
Is it not the unhatched egg before the crack?
That pregnant moment before the Bang?

But then, from Winter's deep lungs,
a cold chant creeps towards the center of things
its ragged hand erasing what
summer had boldly written
and all the lusty leaves gone under

A frozen fist lands like a death-march
threatening to bury even
our too brief afternoons

Everything wants to hide
or dive under the nearest bush

The Looking Away is terrible,
and even the eye of the moon is closed

She's looking after herself now—
even tonight she gazes not upon the land
which sleeps dreamless and cold and alone

Until finally, the world becomes too much with us:
We go to the cave

The secret one, in the dark mountain
seeking safety, a retreat, an inward looking

We've been here before. Many times—
as far back as it will be forever forth
The Big Rhythm holds it all

Within the cave something pulses.
It's why we go there.

We hear it even now
that which deepest dark cannot smother
winter's hands cannot touch
and shadows stalking have no purchase

tender tendrils of our very own vine
bearing the wine of our heart: *in vino veritas*

like embers of eternal vernal
a spark electric, immune to season's scorn
a flame everlasting, a memory

Aha! Some secret vial of our heart's fuel
distilled for this very hour
to sip the season brightly

And the sun too misses his mistress
and cannot too long stay away
He was meant for this: to shine
For to not share his love is a wounding

So in that darkest hour
he knocks on the nearest horizon
and announces The Return:

"Dear Love, I'm Here."

Which is exactly what we find
written on the walls of our cave

as we witness the melting dawn
heralding The Promise

All frozen walls fall
before the mighty glow
we look around and see with new eyes
first breath after coma

and though it's just a whisper now
It is enough to start it all again
and again…again…again…

Juicy Circles

The world is leaking circles again

At dawn you find yourself filling with juice
and your flesh will have to expand.

It's tight in there.

So deliciously tight it hurts with pleasure.

The edges want to feel the kiss of the wind
and be eaten by the next set of lips passing by.

This is the order of things:
Death. Sun. Juice. Circle. Life.

That is a story for the mind.

First fruit whispers:

Start where you are
and stretch into the circle
the Big Juice is trying to be through you.

That is a story for the soul.

Swollen Days

In the swollen days of July
I'm the slow ant

drifting alone across la playa
with a pelican breeze

one grain short of a beach
one sandy soul sunning
just out of reach

I'm an egg huevoneando
learning to cook itself

I'm the río running wide
outside time
Inside the outside-eyed ride

I'm the night enormous
enamored and kissing

the stars scribbling down
a wild wink of a life

spelling me out
in splendiferous form

winks start affairs
and ants build empires

helping to sleep us
under green eye of Venus

Sueña conmigo,
mi amor de la playa

one grain in the sand
igual que yo

sueño contigo
one grain in the sand

let's swell swellingly
and make a beach of it

not just any beach, but one
like a summer dream

Here You Can Laugh in February

Here you can laugh in February

the unexpected is to be expected--
a midnight creature leaves
bay nuts for you
and the creek is singing for its supper

woodpeckers and owls
tell you what time it is
but what about the new birds
that weren't here in dark December?

You might think that February
is dreaming spring,
the equinox on her mind.

It's easy enough to do
but not to get ahead of ourselves
is a good morning task—
February is dreaming February

The season is laughing stinging nettles
and sticky monkeys

the month is grinning meadow flowers
as pink ox eyes at dawn

and yes, a yellow saluting
affirmation of the still slanting sun
inching higher in the sky
day by day by day
like a toddler learning to stand

urging the arroyo willow
and wild currants
to see who can bud best

by the end of the month

and I'm not opposed to opening
my sun-starved belly to it all

skin smiling wildly
with mild stone fruit
freely singing its scent
into the canyon breeze

breathing and breathing

like only second-month California can
see it while you can:
a one-tree performance
of White Petal Extravaganza

as the western wind applauds
and kicks his heels up
to play the eucalyptus
like a harp
and runs his fingers through
Monterey's long pine hair
when he really gets aroused

and they seem to like being tickled
in that way
letting out a moan now and again

as if stretching for the first time
giving one ideas
on a February morning

which is not unlike a thousand other mornings
that have come before
and will come after

But it is

Drinking the Season

November comes to the forest
as an ocean on the head

Something finally dissolves
and a man turns to mist
as struggle takes its leave

Most birds play it safe
but some brave birds still sing
the rain makes the kid in them
get up and dance

Their whistle and the tappity tap tap
on the roof of the 20 square foot hut
are the only sounds

Watch the moss
grow by the minute
greening boulder and bolder yet

Conquering the forest with greenness
and thereby settling it once and for all

Drinking the rain
as the night drinks the dark
and the man drinks the season

YES, BIG SKY

But Listen Skyly

But listen skyly
with moon ears spying
you'll soon as silver
prune it pridely
all the undue dogged doing

unknow it slowly
unown the lying
you'll hear the song-sing
clarifying

your lovely lunar flow-mind brewing

Sometimes Softly Over the Hills the Moon

Sometimes softly over the hills the moon
and sometimes through the pines the vernal wind

often in shapes infinite the clouds
and crowds of ladybugs and people too

daily over the horizon a sun
and under the ruppling creek the newt

and sometimes out of the branch a bud
and out of the well of his soul the man

and sometimes at dusk the dancing,
the people pretending to be coyotes
pretending to be the moon
pretending to be the human
pretending to be the dance

under the moon over the hills
through the silhouette of the pines in the clouds
at the center of the universe, the belonging

sometimes with grace, the coherence of things
where you find yourself
sometimes

The Stars Used to Fall

The stars used to fall
into the eyes of the villagers

Back when the birds sang the morning
like a welcome flood of a new day
and the town rejoiced

The stars used to fall
into the hearts of the villagers

But then the machine came
and its son Power and daughter Speed
chased the stars away
and with them the hushed radiance fled the town

You tell people about that time
and a flicker in the corner
of their jet brown eye
utters, "I think I remember that"

But like a shooting star
it flares and burns out
and the stars in their quiet
glowburn mystery
await the flame in the eyes and hearts
that will bring them back

Because they too miss being seen
and their silent star songs
miss being heard
across the lonely miles

Believe the Sky

Believe the sky
that speaks to you
long lost field of vision

Believe the whispering
red petals in the mud

The hand which holds the lover's—
believe that, but not the grip
that pulls you under

The others will be calling
the voices that take you from your belonging—
don't believe them

they have nothing to do with your task

They are bloated fleas
lost and wasting away
on the poor old dog of your smaller self
and won't survive another moon

Believe the skin of the sky
for the drum you'll beat
in rhythmic desire

Trust the guts within
and their splendid heat
that pull you towards the greater fire

Believe the sky that speaks to you

The way you hear it
is like no other

No Less Than Rain Am I

Not less than rain am I
What thought of flood or mud endured
When flung from ample glandular?

"Secrete!" commands the cloud.
"Release it all and fall to earth,
Unleash your fine and furied mirth."

Of life nor death but both
And that which strikes the heart of it
Through an endless flowing forth

Suck up what can be drunk
Dip your eager, root it swelling.
Yes, sate your dipsomania

Once flung, the deed is done
The wetting fills the gaps still dry
Calm falling from a patient sky

For now, a beat sustained
It is but the mood and form of day
And tends to match her thirstiness

But come the night of storm
When touch is lost with ordered land
No cloud will lend a calming hand:

A mood mercurial to varied motions lend
An amorous discourse earthward bends:

Of sudden pace it abandons form
To whipping gale spinning
Uttering thundered breathless patterns pounding

Lightnings' tonguish flame in wettest
Omni-operant flicked and folded
Orgasmatic undulating inundation!

And meets her gaping, groping
In old and ancient passion play

"Too much! But more!" the ground it cries.
"Our mouths entaste in gulps of you
Let us resting, digest it full."

Then dawn dips in again,
Absorbing night's emissive mission

The land is clear and still
The sky, and I, reposed fulfilled.
A new, fine feature geologe

Not less than she, do I
This etch upon the face of things
Does flow-a river, freshly born

To where she goes, do I
From whence she came, like rain, is round
And wrung from sky spectacular

Yet night is not, but mark
It on its way around again
To give its gust(o)racular

Not less the rain am I
Nor less the wind, and storm unleashed
Obeying throbbing pulsity.
To spend itself again, again

In hallowed-born necessity.

Eclipse

In your uncanny orb of night, join these
Gathered ingredients of earth and sky,
Bold eremite of the winter season.
Blushing argent cheeks with ancient red wine

In the darkling hour of your silent
Transfiguration: Let the pot boil.

Hue with bodies heaving spells the spicy
Concatenation of your churning dish.

Accept the earthly shadow and resist not
The wondrous gravity of the moment.
With light and dark your destined orbit's marked.

Wax gibbous and grow a pregnant shaping
Of some image towards unfurled freedom

From that uncooked root called fear, a toxin
Spreading through the whole like soured liquid

And festering, sinks a sumptuous stew—
The more ingested, the more hunger too.

Now the lunatic transmutation made
Not by magic, nor with wand of wizard
But by channeled heat and moves cathartic.

Stir with patience the hearty blend within
Until all poison into sweetness changed.

Behold a new fruit, orb oracular!
Transliberating itself down the west
By and through and with that which holds it all.

A peach, vigorous belly earthbound bent
And bruised—a mere emblem of its ripeness.

Pluck it from the sky! Break your holy fast
With holy hunger and greet the dawn with
A wild and boisterous jubilance:

Sun in one hand, the moon in the other
With nectar dripping down your canny face.

YES, WIND, YES, WATER

The Perfect Moment Standing Before You

How far did the western wind travel
to meet you here

in this perfect moment
standing before you?

Yet again life begins
and the water is waiting for you

the hot center of the earth
and the star dust cold

conspiring to open
this window to the world

Yet, do you resist
looking through it

with eyes of dawn
and a radiant heart?

Trade in your stiff eyes
and join the wild wind

The Wind Is Its Own Authority

Have you ever tried to push the wind?

Wind is its own authority
bearing its gifts
with ferocity and tenderness
in equal measure

It may steal your house
no matter how many nails you own
It will pollinate your field
no matter how many fences you
It will take the strongest tree
to the earth
A regeneration
through destruction

It will kiss your cheek
until you blush
regardless of how you try to turn away
bringing you
the vital living breath

Learn this from the wind:

Unchain your own voice
sing the song of the earth
take your breath
at your own pace
and give it back
to the Big Circulation

Of Wind and Water

It's surprising how little gets
done without them—
just try dancing without the dark blood
of the earth
coming up through your bones
as red sea water

or the rivers of wind
warmed by the sun
snaking through you creaturely

The wind carries its own center
with it across the miles
adding a ring with each breath

It is always en route
sparking conversations
with skin and scale
leaf and litter

When you think you've arrived
ask the wind and the water

When you know you haven't arrived
and the labyrinth seems too big
ask the wind and the water

They are the peacekeeper
and the destroyer
The life-giver and the blood of the big body
The crack in the bell
The crack in the ego

The weight and the lack of it
draw them through the endless cycle

To ask where it begins
misses the point

Not the hydrogen nor oxygen
but the bond that brings
the thousand forms

The kind of bond you want
when you want to have a dialogue
about the shape of things
When you want to bring soul to the world

When you want to introduce the sea to the mountain
to offer parts of yourself
you haven't seen in years
to the parts you haven't even met

The parts of yourself
you thought were a virus
so you fought them off
like a valiant, but confused soldier

thinking that it's best to be safe
you forgot that nothing is outside the circle

Thinking for a moment you were
not the same center as the wind
you forgot the thundering imperative
of your audacious body

The bond that breathes you
in and out, in and out
carries its own center
at the edge of things

How to Disappear Into the River

I don't wanna see the river
don't wanna even tell you about it

I wanna drink myself so far into it

I stop making sense
because I breathe it
from the inside out
sucking down the mountaintop
and spitting into the sea

Squeaking like a swallow
until a flock of rocks falls
out of my banks
and something in me hears the shoreline giggle—
Did she mean to touch up against me like that?

Catch the light, carry the wind
test the world's ear
rewrite the land
with my side-winding snake of a thousand hearts

Not delicate, but deluge
not going somewhere new
but creating somewhere new

Growing the fish and fisherwoman
the poet pelican otter man
inside my river womb
Abraq ad habra

Swim in me—
I'll drown you safely
to the other side

I chant river forever forever
not to show off for the water birds
though yes that too

but because I'm full
and overflowing

I sing wet my wild
singing yet the while
forever foriver
Singing river river

Until these wicked words
evaporate
in the slow of deep July
and I with them
disappearing
into the flow

How Would You Ever Meet?

Be honest—
if you couldn't tell where the tip
of the feather ended
and the skin of your eye began
it wouldn't be a river
and you wouldn't be a man
and these words wouldn't be a fish
swimming between you two
and you wouldn't feel the pelican
pulling you into the ripples

So how would you ever meet?

Only the Wind

There's something down there
waiting to live

But at this burnt hour
before the tired sun
hides behind the hills

I feel only the wind.

At first a flirt
with hairs on hands
a dance across my chest

and then, the best:
a stinging kiss on my cheek.

Off it goes
playing through the dry rattlesnake grass
searching for its next romance.

The wait is over.

I'm alive.

YES, PLAY

Jump In Me

A ten-year old boy
stands atop a concrete bridge
on a dusty rural road
under a simmering Iowa sun
kissing his skin red

The cold creek below beckons:
jump in me

He jumps with abandon.

A 44-year old man
stands on a sandy bank of a cold river
under a sweltering California sun
kissing his skin red

All his skin cells have been replaced
many times over
but his heart remains the same

The 10-year old boy beckons:
jump in me

He jumps with abandon.

'Shroom Forest

If I were shrunk
and found myself
the size of a seed

I'd build a home among the 'shrooms
in a village called *Puhpowee*—
the Potawatomi word
for the force which causes mushrooms
to push up from the earth overnight

I'd wake and wash my face
in the dew drop
that collected on my mushroom cap roof
every morning

and would hold little gatherings
among the grandmother grove of mushrooms
with an altar of spores
and even tinier seeds
of every stripe and hue

And we'd have a little fire
which we'd start
with a single redwood needle
twice my size

So I'd need to find
a nice 'shroomy girl
to help me break it down
and light it

Then all us fungi villagers
would sing mushroom songs

around the tiny flame—
folksy songs about lichen and love
and what it would be like to
be big like a fern
among the giant redwood trees

and after the fire died down
some of us would stay behind
and tell stories about our first time

About sneaking into Mr. Psilo's
big mushroom mansion
and how he was bald-headed by age 30
saying how we hope we never got that old

But if we did, well, we'd promise each other
we'd stay young at heart
and always caper about in the woods together

and never, *ever* get so old
that we wouldn't stick our bare feet
in the cold creek
on the soft ground
and put our arms around
each other in mushroom tree homes.

That's what I'd do
if I were the size of a seed.

*Puhpowee is from Robin Wall Kimmerer's gorgeous and inspiring book, *Braiding Sweetgrass: Indigenous Wisdom, Scientific Knowledge and the Teachings of Plants*. Potawatomi is a member of the Anishinaabe language family

Quailitos

I went to pick blackberries
and found a covey of quail
a mama and her little ones
looking quite feathery frail

A question mark crest dangled
above their quailish eyes
and exclamation points marked
their crisp and chirpy cries

I plucked a juicy berry
and tossed it on my tongue
then plucked a chirpy chirp
from the charming song they sung

They marched to a rhythm
both quaint and quirky fun
and took a dusty bath
in the summer sun

I chewed on the chirpy chirps
less chunky than chill and bright
until mama quail led her chicks
into the warm and quiet night

YES, CREATE

Weave Your Outrageous Image

You see, they must put things
in between you and your thread

How else can they recruit you
to sew up *their* dream?
Without the mounds of dirt
thrown over your warp and woof

how could you become the face
of forgetfulness
and follow someone else's thread?

Jog your memory:
there can be *nothing* in between
that you do not allow

Your one holy precept:
Do not abandon thy luminous thread

Get clear of the dirt
and take the thread in your hand

They will see your wondrous thing
and will understand

or not.

They may cast twisted eyes
laughing
or empty blinking silence
upon your vast design

or even banish you—but only from the houses
to which you don't belong.

It matters not.

Because some,
by seeing your intricate threading,
will begin to forget
their own forgetting

and you, my friend,
can weave again
your outrageous image into the world

Don't Be Quiet About Beauty

My friend, don't be quiet about beauty
don't be silent about love
don't seal your lips quite yet

Even the ones who think it's quaint
and queer, this talk unconstrained
even the ones loudest and preening
ache for love and beauty
through miles of debris

Oh, everyone talk of roots
but I say, grow past the ones they gave you
past the names that call you
past the farthest sideways glance

Let them follow their own trajectory
like lonely reckless heroes
seeking the sacred well
let them dig, so you can fly

Keep digging and seize your true name
from the center of the earth

Then rise up north by northwest
until the secret shakes itself out—
clean and heroic green
finally yelling,

yes, yes,
I want that too!

Then sing the beauty of the whole mystery

Take Up Your Wand

"If one uses a baton, the baton itself must be a living thing, charged with a kind of electricity, which makes it an instrument of meaning in its tiniest movement."
—Leonard Bernstein

It matters not the noise of the crowd.

How might that mindless cacophony
even approach your perfect pitch?

Let the noise be a Nothingness to you.

Chop off your ears, if you must, Maestro,
and hear the charm of the music
born of bones within

Take up your wand in hands majestic molded
and conduct your own sacred symphony

Stir the oboes from their solemn slumber
put to sleep by the loud trumpeters,
roguish assassins of the soul

Pick up your baton, Blessed Conductor

Let your left hand be
the rhythm of the dusk and dawn
and your right hand
be the freedom of a supernova

Be the author of your own notes
and between them
pour your solar-panoramic audacious breath

Strange Birds

They are strange birds
perched on the shoreline

these heavy poets chirping lightly
for whom squares will not do.

They are in it for the curves only.

The shoreline keeps shape-shifting—
that is the key to the rest.

It is a sentinel against forgetting
and if you don't understand the shoreline
how can you understand the human heart?
they say.

So they perch on the Pacific
purchasing poems
with their spindrift ears

Sometimes they fall on their head
listening to the vast subterranean love-beats

Building things

for the hawk within, stone towers
for the multitudes within, stone benches
for the child within, feather ships

Between dinner and desert
a drop from the great voyage
drips on a napkin
and still we clean our chins with it

Scribbling scribbling

on the black island
in the storm
in the crowd
on the sea
in the trenches of a world asunder
in the mines
from the glowburn night
on the backs of whales

the music wafts in from every direction
and the notes are untranslatable

Yet we hunger for syllables of understanding

How curious that petal-soft verse
is sometimes harder than granite

and holds us up
like a fat bird on an ocean gale

Chirp chirp for us you strange birds
with sounds carved from rocks and flesh
and all the slight angles
of our ancient dispositions

Chirp your inimitable chirp
you strange birds

Chirp chirp and make our flesh
cha cha with goosebumps

YES, WILD ONE

Coyote Moments

You look familiar
we said to each other
emerging from oaks and vetch
and rattlesnake grass.

It was just barely the kiss of the morning
her big ears were up
and so we're mine,
eyes round with wonder.

The ears of the oaks
and eyes of the rattlesnake grass
remained the same.
The vetch watched in curiosity.

You're different than I thought, I said.

Her reddish-grey coat caught the morning light
and she replied,
You're different than I thought.

We were tempted by habit
to replay an old script—
skittish and wary, averting eyes,
running towards safety.

But instead, the ever new wind
danced through the limbs of the oak
and the rattlesnake grass
and the spiraling arms
of purple vetch stretching.

and because our ears were up
we heard it

One or the both of us
began singing:

"You're so beautiful...

I like you...

I want to know you..."

And so we stayed
sharing moments in the wind
as new friends
in the kiss of the morning light.

Owl Saint of Night

A great hunger arises
from the center of things

crickets howl at dusk
amidst the peace

at the edge of the meadow
a cold hoot stands sentinel

seeking satisfaction
along the perimeter

rabbit bows her head
in quiet ceremony

safe from shadows swinging
down without a sound

Oh Owl Saint of Night
feathered rhythm in furtive flight

knives from killer sky
piercing jugular, jumping
screaming bunny, heaving
high-pitch horror, bleeding
body kicking, raining
remains of rabbit
dying into darkness, flying

Final thoughts such as these:

"Hope is not the thing with feathers,
and for all the feathers fine
a bitter chill it was,
the bitter chill was mine."

The curtain closes with a hoot
on an ancient afternoon

Artemis smiles from the east
a winter silence resumes

Call Me By My Name Ornate

Dedicated to Caddisfly larvae

From the outside
I may look like a clumsy tumbling acrobat
dragged across the bottom of things
by lawless currents

but those gold flakes you see
the ones woven through my back—
those I found in the basement of life

where the shed skin of mighty mountains
and delicious detritus live
awaiting their new forms in me

I spiral pink granite
and coil chips obsidian around myself
and make a home of it

call me by my name ornate
or not at all
my cave is cast-off sedimental sentiment

plucking lucky earth
vulnerable to the elements
and resurrected in me
as Goldworthy-worthy art

until the sun pops my feathery wings
and I carve a mansion among the clouds

sipping ambrosial air
like a poet and his words
drunk on draughts of light
and buzz madly like a riot

Why Should I Write About You, Water Bug?

When the heavens are rolling out encores
of mulberry processions
and the river is performing not-stop
a cappella hits

Why should I write about you, water bug?

While the elegant bats somersault
in dusky diners
and the thunderstorm breaks its head
on distant peaks

what have you to say to me, six-footed floater?

Then, I see you flash and slide
and if I didn't see it with my own two eyes
the way you disappear
only to reappear two inches upstream
I'd be inclined to think I was dreaming

and for the life of me
I don't know what you eat
so I can only assume it is water and air alone

but now I know better

You are an advanced species
of micro-teleportation devices and magic
hydrophobic microhairs
dancing the river down
with sophisticated water choreography

not tiny and insignificant
in the scheme of things

but the whole show—
the entire mountain and sun extravaganza—
is for you

the moon-rise
the coyote rips
the distant storm
and towering pines bow
to your practiced patience
and river spells

That is why, water monk,
I write about you
and join them in the worship

YES, DARKNESS

Shadow Shining

I. soil

in humble black gold
like downtrodden lifting all
seeds dreaming green
sleep like sparks in womb of the dark

II. sky

in longest night
when tulips aren't even on the tip of a dream
cold creeps towards the center
of a hibernating winter heart
where a lowly sun is born
whispering secrets

III. silhouette

in the stretched pregnant hour
before the dance of day
this hushed unrushed unseen hanging chill
clings a damp cloak
skin tight on the fog face hymn of owl
while stars sing soliloquies

IV. soul

in pitch black sacred wound
that sharp deep ancient ache
your darkness shines
a gorgeous throbbing face
a lighthouse calling you to the shoreline
of homecoming

The Moon Has a Long Memory

Welcome dark
in unpursed lips singing
forget the day
all pale doing

of center night
and darklish wooing
lay its leaping skin
around you

Deep nocturnal breath abiding
blowing skirt of darkness hiding
Welcome dark
in unpursed lips singing

The moon has a long memory
and hasn't forgotten your true name

It is mere habit to shrink
when the sun sinks

Have you tried standing up
and meeting the gaze of the Swordsman
when he asks you what luster's tucked under
your supernova skin?

Have you considered lifting the lid
off your day-time self
stitched tight oh too tight and oh—

Or are you only a lover of butterflies
despiser of bats?

One of the half-time lovers of the world?

Then by all means, bless your mangled life
half-bitten and hungry

If not, pour pitch black down your poor back
and feel your arch grow

The moon has a long memory
and hasn't forgotten your name

the one you uttered so assuredly
back in the season of jumping
before the great gremlins of approval
stole it from you
with foggy breath

Be big with midnight
and tempt the stars out
with Cheshire desire

Behold, some bold belly cries your full name
deeplier than ever
Perhaps it is your own

Welcome dark
in unpursed lips singing
forget the day
all pale doing

of center night
and darklish wooing
lay its leaping skin
around you

YES, LOVE

Love on the Table

You recall a cabin on the edge of town
in woods of alder and oak

There were big windows on every side
and a porch stretched around
like a loose-fitting belt
just barely keeping things in

sometimes it was a stepping stone to the world
and sometimes it was a moat keeping things out

You recognize it because it was your house
and a life was built there once upon a time

And on the porch you recall there was an old table
crooked, but round and steady

And Love was on the table resting shiningly
and whenever the front door cracked open
it flooded in like dawn

Sometimes you noticed—other times not

Each morning you raced to all the Theres
trying to earn your belongingess
of an eager world wanting proof

And when you returned later
the porch and the table were still there

and when you cracked the door
to the home you built

sometimes you noticed
the light pouring in and sometimes not

When dusk settled in for its daily prayer
Love became the moon
illuminating parts of the cabin
that even the sun can't reach

and flowed through the window
silhouetting a figure curled up
before the fireplace—
a dog or a wolf—
your memory isn't clear

But then a particular morning came
after a long, winter night—
that kind that is both cold and cozy
and full of memories and rest and safety—
a morning that greeted you differently than others.

You remember because the door wouldn't close
and after a while you didn't want it to close

and abhorring a vacuum
the light couldn't help itself
and went swimming through all the rooms

and instead of rushing to all
the Theres of the world
you paused on the porch
noticing something out of the corner of your soul

And pulling a chair
up to that crooked table

you broke your fast
and had a morning meal with Love

I'm a Dream You Had Under the Moon

I'm just a dream you had
A night your soul spent with the trees
playing under the moon

I was the creek falling through you
so you could feel your own flow

I became night so you could share your darkness
and say the big secrets out loud
and not merely have them echo on the canyon walls

I was the uprooted tree in the shape
of a falcon's talon
for you to be caught and released

you slipped right between them

Oh, how good that felt—
It was all over your face

I was the path for you to go ahead on

With eyes of night
I became the path ahead
to protect you from the Predator

I was the fallen redwood needle
growing from the middle
as my hands danced with yours
dancing with me being the needle

The old does not always fall away
before the new appears

I became the moon
and showed you half my face
so you could see your own

The half you want the world to see
is the half the world needs

The other half will be another dream.

Not of me, but in being more you by dreaming me.
By dreaming me seeing you

Me holding you. You holding yourself.

That feeling, a playful poem in the dirt.

That is all within you. Don't ask why or interpret it.

I'm what your soul is trying to be in the world.
Your blind-spot being seen.

I will come out and play as your dream
whenever you need it.

That is what I do
Until you find me in the bottom of your bones
as your truest image

When you don't need to dream me anymore
you will wake up and find me gone.

Astonished, you will turn over
and embrace the love
that's always been there.

YES, GRIEF

At What We've Done

What sign has been flung
when even ravens hold their tongue?

Left their pranks in trees to hang
and even wolves have lost their fang?

What tumult has begun
when all the warnings have been rung?

When spring has sprung
but all the bees have been stung?

When every alarm's already sung?

Even the stones stand stunned
at what we've done.

At what we've done.

Gone

"If we have become incapable of denying ourselves anything, then all that we have will be taken from us." –Wendell Berry, *Leavings*

All but the one redwood.

Took only 15 years—
an entire forest of giants vanished
in a single breath

Hills scraped clean
like a quick shave

Stubbled and stunned
to build the places we love—called Oakland
Martinez, Benicia, Lafayette
San Francisco cable cars

Grandchildren circle around the stumps
tiny compared to the mighty ones

32 feet in diameter
bigger than any ever known

But one remains as...a reminder? A ghost?
A dream?

*From 1845-1860 all the original giant redwoods in the San Francisco Bay Area were cut down for lumber to build the surrounding cities, except one: "Old Survivor" or "Grandfather" is the only old growth redwood tree in the East Bay, more than 400 years old. It still stands in Oakland's Leona Heights Park.

No Shiny Hope

I. Bruises

I'm not going to speak of shiny hope today
it has troubled us for too long
tripping us down the stairs
leaving the bruises that stick around

We want to jump over truth
straight to hope
bought in the marketplace of shadows

It's not surprising it has no legs
and collapses
as soon as it gets out of bed

We can't get there without touching the ground

II. Let us stop jumping

To stop running chasing filling
filling filling filling filling filling filling filling filling filling filling

stop.

and then, if grief and all its cousins
should arrive
trying to suffocate you in your sleep
embrace them like long lost loved ones

III. When the lights turn off

Will we stumble?

Or will we have learned to believe
in our own breath
and the dirt under our feet?

Will we have practiced how to say hello?

All the beautiful things await.

IV. Something sturdier than shiny hope

Your own dawn looking earth in the face
saying, "I remember you"

Start crawling.

Mix the kernel of your true heart—that improbable spark
in the vastness—
with the clay of where you live
deep with dreams

YES, CONNECTION

Where Shall We Find Each Other?

When I say, "The mushrooms are doing pushups,
the madrones are dancing happy,
and the dawn is smiling smilingly,"

It is a fact.
Because I say so.

And when you say, "Actually,
trees are rooted, so they can't dance
and they can't be happy,
because they don't have minds,
you are projecting. And besides,
smilingly is not a word,
and even if it is, you're being redundant,"

It is a fact.
Because you say so.

When I say "A butterfly is a silently
floating pyramid of Original Dust,
ancient wingéd atom,"

and you say, "Actually,
atoms are the basic building blocks of matter,
consisting of protons, neutrons, and electrons,
and even smaller units called quarks,"

We must then consult THE ENCYCLOPEDIA of FINAL
OBJECTIVITY
because I don't see blocks or units,
and you don't see wings.

So then we say, "Perhaps we can't be friends anymore,

because I don't know where you live,
nor you, I.

How shall we find each other?"

But I need you. And you, I.

Where is the Directory of our Imaginations
that shall tell us where to meet?

Dream a Constellation

Tell me, do they have periwinkle sunsets
in the land where you live?

Was there a river in your childhood
that flows through your dreams?

Shall we fight over which river is better
and who owns the sun?

Or shall we tell stories
around the fire

and balance our souls along the banks
while the day is pulling her shades down

and the stars that no one knows
begin to dot our mutual horizon?

Perhaps someday we will dream
a constellation together

and it will matter not
whether I call it the Great Blue Heron

or you call it the Giant Spruce
or our sister calls it the Goddess Ostara

for in that day,
the sun will shine on us both

and the stars will guide our nights
filled with better tales

Unscheduled Grace

This will not reduce the confusion
as if it's a map at the station entrance
showing you where to get off

and the names of things
speeding by on time

it assumes we're going
where we're all headed

it is loud and crowded
on this train. as the doors close

some people are left behind
and we lurch forward

old shoes shiny shoes
coats of winter, perfume

tired eyes, vacant eyes
eyes that want to know

somehow a butterfly has boarded
lost, I suppose, perhaps afraid

the eyes of two strangers
smile with one another

seeing the unannounced beauty
rest on another stranger's hat

a morning miracle
on the Millbrae

even though it throws its body
against the dark window

it cannot see the charm
of its own pomegranate red

and lacy black
delicate darting

its wings are not ornamental now
but means of escape

the eyes of more strangers
light up, flitting here and there

without their permission, their faces
do wonderful things not forced

and for a moment
they make a dwelling together

on the common ground
of an unscheduled grace

Gossamer Threads

Gossamer threads
string together the world

some seen
some unseen

follow the ones that draw you
towards the face of dawn

the threads keep leaping
silently like a spider

blade to blade
heart to heart

mud to star
rock to wet rock

through the fog
on the big river

one foot in front of the other
over the water with big green trust

follow the ones that pull
your soul out

and tug your monumental heart
steady through the thousand turns

YES, MYSTERY

Stepping Stones

I am not the one you are looking for
but a stepping stone for you
to find the one you are
(It/she/he/we said to each other)

you are closer than you think
as the water washes over me/you/us

we trade moments being the stone
and see how easy it is to get confused

and think that you are trying
to get to the other side
when you are really the Water Itself

see the rock and the one stepping
as your left and right eye

and with your other Eye
view both shores and the river
that flows between them

as your vastness cracking
into the deep well

Something Draws You Out

The poem you live inside of
is not much different
than a walk in the forest

Something draws you out

Perhaps you know what
or perhaps you do not

But there you are
one foot in front of the other
drawn forward
like a migrating buffalo
across the continent
of your butterfly soul

syllable after syllable
wrangled wordward and woodward

watching, you catch a glimpse
of something flying
from out of the corner of your self

the way the magnolia lives
as a scent on the wind

and you make it a part
of your body

the way a true poem lives
beyond the borders of the words

and the moon moves among the branches
as a mysterious midnight dancer

Something in you knows
the true walk is happening
between each step

like the creek's echoes
rushing beyond its banks
to join the promenade
among the shadows

To find who cast them
is one reason you left your house
to walk in the first place

The other reasons only you know
and the world is waiting to hear

But the slower the pace,
the more the walk
the slower the pace
the more the poem

stepping into you
with each fall of your foot

and the moment between each
a wintry space is born
from the same place as the wind
where no one knows

Oh, if winter comes, can the spring in your steps
be far behind?

Suddenly, you've 'taken' a walk
with each springy footfall
having no choice
but to speak its blossoms

You've reached the end of the winter poem
you've been hearing, and the trail ends

You forget the midnight cold
because now summer is a dream
on the lips of your feet
creating a new trail
with each new dreamprint

You could interpret a walk
asking, 'what does it mean?'

but it's a question asked backwards
up the hill

If the meaning could be told,
why, just stay at home and let the forest be

Your feet will be innocent and happy.

But you must know your poem will find other ways of being heard.

It has taken _you_—
the walk.
The poem.

The seasons spin you
and a conversation has begun.

What the Whole World Is Trying To Be

With this hand I touched the skin of a madam madrone
her silky red winter blush
bending spring-ward through the fog

And with this hand I reached into the water
cold with the taste of seasons
scooping the mud that had waited all year
to feel my face

A lavender whistle petaled into me
like a feather from an unseen canopy
as the bright alphabet of dawn
uttered itself deliciously into my ear

Someone who had my hands
became a mud person
unlocking an image within

and the great tree awoke, remembering a dream:

That it had been a man standing on the banks of a creek
one hand on a madrone
the other full of mud
and wondered at having five-twigged hands
and moving so quickly from rock to rock

Then, shaking this strange image from its limbs
got up and stretched, saying,

I am what the whole world is trying to be

and washed its face in the morning mist

Old Beauty Born of the Pulse

Do you believe in liberation?

Think about it hard.

No, don't think at all.
What shape do the lips of your fourth stomach make?

How you answer determines which direction
the face of your slippery heart turns
when the birds wake you from slumber

You don't have to choose between the sky
and the dirt.

The green was built from sunlight for you.

Raven sits on the tree-top telling the other birds
and ground creatures when the stranger is approaching.

But the red-shouldered hawk above
cuts an arc of light
with his invisible scythe
catching the currents
telling the world there are no strangers

He is the stranger to whom nothing is strange.

Those feathers that tickle your heart in the morning
are the same feathers that poke your eye out
when the black spot descends on your back
and the great scream is liberated from your warm body

They are the same feathers
you dip in the ink to write your life

They are the same feathers
that adorns the wild wings
of a surprised world

The ones it borrows to be the new beauty
which is the old beauty
born of the pulse

The pulse in that fourth stomach of yours.

The Hand Inside You

This way is not what you think.

It makes some want to grab it
and others hide in caves

Where are those who dare it?

To look in its eyes and withstand the mighty gaze
without being knocked down?

Or if knocked down,
relish it for what it teaches, teaching itself

It is not what you suppose—
it cannot be grabbed nor hid from

Stand in the bright light and absorb the shadow

There is no secret—
It is written in blue daylight
as much as the black skies and green meadows

Every rock and cloud spells it
and you find it at the bottom of every eye
every weed and putrid habit

Hold the hand inside you to find out

No fear can breathe
when it recognizes itself
from the inside
all the beautiful things

YES, STILLNESS

The Silence Beyond

I sit at the feet of the tall ones
apprenticing to redwoods
to learn an ancient dialect

Sitting in circle:
Grandmother teaches stillness
Owl sings lullabies
Bird tells stories
Creek teaches flow

In time, the chirps settle down
gurgles fall away
even that high-pitched tale
from the treetop of my head—
that strange frenzy—loses all energy

The canyon is at peace.

Yet even beyond that
in the cave behind the waterfall
is the language of Deep Time
where even words of wisdom
are distant echoes on the wall

In the grammar of stillness
a patient heart seed takes a cosmic breath
and I hear something
closer than my own heartbeat:

The silence beyond

Beyond Fences, A Meadow

Somewhere there is a meadow
beyond fences and the thousand rattles

that breathes in mountain air
and breathes out fuchsia flowers

and from the edge one can watch
the world ceasing up

in all its fearful loneliness
through the seven seasons

and all its striving
like a child for its mother

grasping towards the toy
that got away behind the curtain

but the meadow up there
it keeps meadowing
butterflies and wild onions

effortlessly, and effortlessly
the clouds come and go
in the big cerulean sky

where music lives
before the first note is born

and stillness that is midwife
to the storm goes to keep her peace

and all the colors
become their true selves

before the shadow
suffers their shine

somewhere there is the green meadow
just beyond the next peak

or perhaps it's at the foot of the peak
that stands before you now

behind all the pretty fences
that you yourself put up

EXCERPTS FROM RYAN VAN LENNING'S NEWEST BOOKS

From his collection of haiku, *High-Cooing Through the Seasons*

Like that maple leaf
in the cool autumn midnight—
hard time letting go

*

Just a few days old
and walking across the sky—
my new baby moon

*

Going for a walk
enjoy your mid-day orgy
lovely ladybugs

*

Forest asks at dusk:
"What does loneliness look like?"
Cottonwood's last leaf

*

Traveled so far, then
got tangled up in the pines—
mountain mistiness

*

Coastal breeze at dusk
cormorant offers night class:
sit and dry your wings

138

From *Headwaters and Heartrocks*, Ryan Van Lenning's forthcoming collection of poems, capturing the beauty, flow, and mystery of the encounter with California's rivers and mountains.

HOW THE RIVER DOVE LIKE A FALCON

Tell me more about the river,
son of sun

and you, she of moon,
tell me how the river dove like a falcon
into the new light
not for the kill
but for the joy of soaring
and in the plunge, created the world
once and for all

with silver lips say again
how with wave tips bright as birdlet wings
caught your father's eye
and sliding, pulled it into the day singing
unstoppable and plent with flow
unpenting itself like fate
spending itself into the vastness

about the relentless, curved descent
all fine-whorled and wet

how without reputation or brag
sailed itself like royalty
owning all the lands

and how you stood there
dazzled with delight and full
falling and falling again
through the unburdened talons

INNER CIRCLE OF REDWOODS

Deep gratitude to my biggest supporters, who saw promise in my poetic voice, and without whom this project would have been much more difficult. But just as important, these wild nature hearts made it fun and soulful.

Diane Dew

Katie Baptist

Ariana Candell

Karen Sindelar

Christine Broz

Amirah Schwartz

Kevin Boyd & Jenn Guitart

Aaron & Ashley Thomas

Cyndy Abbott

Cory Van Lenning

Sue Ites

ABOUT THE AUTHOR

Ryan Van Lenning, M.A., is also author of *High-Cooing Through the Seasons*. His new collection, *Headwaters and Heartrocks*, will be released in Winter 2018. Ryan's poetry appears in various poetry journals and the forthcoming book *A Walk with Nature: Poetic Encounters that Nourish the Soul* by University Professors Press. He has published articles in *Earth Island Journal, Truthout,* and *Deep Times: A Journal of the Work That Reconnects*.

Ryan is Co-Founder of Wild Nature Heart, guiding wilderness journeys and facilitating authentic re-connections with nature and our deepest selves to assist in the work of repairing broken belonging. He is a certified ecotherapist through The Earthbody Institute.

He lives outside in the rich redwood and bay forest of the East Bay hills, the wild oaks along the American and Mad Rivers, and the pines of the Sierra mountains.

ABOUT WILD NATURE HEART

Wild Nature Heart supports people to connect with the wisdom of wild nature, to claim their authentic adulthood by showing up as their truest selves, and to live their soul callings and heart stories into the world.

We offer nature connection and creativity workshops, multi-day soul-rooted wilderness journeys and weekend retreats, individual nature-based mentoring, and wilderness vision quests.

We work primarily in the Northern California area, including Oakland/Berkeley, Sacramento, Humboldt County, Santa Cruz mountains, Yosemite, and Grass Valley.

www.wildnatureheart.com

Made in the USA
Lexington, KY
07 December 2019